Divorce is Not for Dummies

How to Cover Your Assets

Nancy A. Hetrick

MAFF®, CDFA™, AWMA™

Copyright © 2015 by Nancy A. Hetrick

ISBN: 978-1519356949

First Printing: December, 2015

Published by 102nd Place LLC
Scottsdale, AZ 85266

Dedication

For my mother who was too
frightened to leave.

Table of Contents

PREFACE

In 2007, after 16 years of marriage, I found out my husband was having an affair. It felt as though my arms and legs had been torn from my body and rammed down my esophagus where they settled in my chest resulting in heaviness I was sure would never go away. (Thankfully it did.)

Despite this reeling emotional betrayal when the time came to file for divorce, I was determined to complete the process with honor and respect. I was grateful for the years we had spent together, the children we had raised together, and the growing up that we had both done – together. Later, much later, I recognized that I had changed dramatically and his affair was only a symptom of the distance that had grown between us. It was best for both of us to move on.

He was consumed with guilt over the affair and had not yet really let go of our marriage and was proposing ridiculous things like "Gee, you should get a house right next door to me so we can still feel like a family!" Yeah, right. I'll just come over and make cookies with your mistress. NOT!

Still, he was being cooperative so we decided that we would do a "do-it-yourself divorce" where I would put together all of the paperwork and file a consent decree, meaning we agreed on everything. It sounded simple: respectful. This could work! Sigh . . . I was so ignorant.

So I put together a basic decree with the help of the Arizona Superior Court Self-Service website. It was a decree that didn't really have any firm rules in it. We had committed to "work together for the best for the kids." Ok, cool.

We had two investment properties and our family home. He kept the home and one rental and I took the other rental with the agreement that we would both refinance our respective properties before the end of the year. Sure.

That was spring of 2007. I refinanced mine. He didn't. The housing market collapses. He ultimately lets BOTH properties fall into foreclosure. With my name on the mortgages, my credit was trashed and there was not one single thing I could do about it because there was nothing in the decree stating our agreements.

About four weeks after the divorce was final his guilt turned to anger, as guilt often does. Now the overriding emotion is anger and he starts dictating when I can and can't see my children. He demands that they switch schools to be closer to him so he doesn't have to drive as far. I begin to realize the huge error I made in not having a divorce decree that I could use to enforce our agreements. So – back to court!

$12,000 later and pages and pages of angry, venomous emails to me, I finally had a court-ordered parenting plan that was enforceable. It didn't help at all with the properties. All I could do was force him to sell once they were worth the appraised value. Gosh that shouldn't take long at all. Sigh . . . He stopped paying on them the following month. For crying out loud, I'm a financial advisor! How did I let this happen? Simple: I was trying to be NICE!

This is one of the biggest mistakes people make. You have ONE CHANCE to do it right. I really should have known better and part of me did, but it didn't help me avoid the financial pitfalls that showed up.

Shortly after my divorce, I became aware of a national credential available to experienced financial advisors specializing in the financial issues around divorce. It's called the CDFA™, Certified Divorce Financial Analyst. Wow, I could help other people not make the same mistakes I did.

I spent the next six months studying and preparing for four different exams for the credential and at the same time had the opportunity to break away from a big corporation and launch out on my own. I became an independent advisor, started my own company, and launched Smarter Divorce Solutions. One thing I learned for sure, Divorce is NOT for Dummies! Let's get smart together.

I've included in this book several of the tools and resources I use in my practice with my clients. Don't worry, this WON'T be a textbook. I know that if you're going through divorce, the last thing you need is a bunch of cold, sterile, data. This book is from-the-gut-no-bullshit REAL. I might even get you to laugh a little. I know, it's a stretch, but I'm going to try.

All my best,

Nancy

CHAPTER 1 – FIRST THINGS FIRST

When you fell in love and got married, you never imagined that your relationship could drift so far from those initial feelings. What was once love, respect, and admiration, has morphed into something unrecognizable and even dysfunctional. Regardless of how or why it ended up this way, there are some things to think about before you make the monumental decision to divorce.

BEFORE You Decide on Divorce!

First and foremost, have you done everything you can? None of us get married with the expectation that it will come to an end. To avoid future regret, make sure that you have done everything you know how to do to save your marriage. Have you sat your spouse down and been brutally honest about how you feel, what you're thinking and what you need? If not, ask yourself if it is fair to expect them to know. Have you insisted on seeing a counselor? When you do, be ready to commit to giving 100% of yourself to the process.

If you are convinced that the relationship is irretrievably broken, then the next step is to start thinking about your future: specifically for the purpose of this book, your financial future. Understand that the same money that supported one household will now have to support two and you will likely BOTH have to take a drop in your standard of living. Think carefully about what you will be able to afford and consider meeting with a financial planner, ideally a CDFA™, Certified Divorce Financial Analyst, to evaluate your options and look at what potential settlements could mean for your future.

If you are not 100% clear on your financial situation, now's the time to get prepared. You must be fully informed about your household finances. It will be very difficult to plan for the next phase of your life if you have no idea how much money you'll have or how much it will cost you to live. A financial planner or CDFA™ can be a very valuable resource for you at this time.

Build a support network. The next 6 months to a year will be one of the most difficult times of your life. Surround yourself with people that will love and support you without being judgmental. You'll need all the support you can get. Take a deep breath and take one step at a time. You WILL get through this.

It's no secret that over 50% of marriages end in divorce; even more if you're on a 2nd or 3rd marriage. Whether this is a good thing or a bad thing depends on your perspective. I believe divorce is often a good thing but that's because I grew up in a family with domestic violence and a mother who believed she could not get out without jeopardizing her children's futures and her own.

Looking back at the time, the early 1970's, I think she was probably right. She may not have received much support at all from my father and there weren't any resources available to us. My sisters and I once called an emergency hotline and were warned that if we made a report, we would likely be removed to four different foster homes.

That was the end of us trying to take action. Fortunately today, support agencies and resources are available to empower women so we aren't forced to remain in a bad situation.

On the other hand, people just quit too darn easily sometimes. Marriage for some has become a partnership of convenience that is only maintained as long as it's fun. "What? It's not always fun? Well the heck with this then. I have lots of other choices." Hmmmm, the grass is not always greener my friend . . . . But hey! Sometimes it absolutely is!

For myself, and even though I didn't feel this way at the time, I understand now that divorce was the best thing that ever happened to me. I've often wondered if humans were really intended to mate for life. When I think of how much I changed from age 20 to age 40, I'm not sure it was fair to expect my spouse to a) keep up with me and b) change in the same direction.

Well obviously it didn't happen and we ultimately made each other miserable. Remember this, if you are not happy in your marriage, I guarantee you your spouse isn't either. He/she may be in total denial about this, but they are not as happy as they could be.

I believe strongly that you only get one chance at this life and it's up to us not to waste any time. I also believe in personal responsibility. If my husband isn't nice enough to me, I know now that the answer is to be nicer to him. If my husband isn't affectionate enough with me, then I become more affectionate to him. If I am not getting enough romance then I plan a romantic dinner. I will never again blame my spouse for my state of mind. That's all mine.

However, if I do all those things on a regular basis and I am met with anger, resentment, detachment, refusal to partici-pate, or no intimacy, then I have a decision to make, don't I. If I ask my spouse to see a counselor with me and he refuses – well that should tell me a lot. My life is short and I will NOT sacrifice it for someone who chooses to be miserable.

So now what?

The reality for many couples that have been married for 10 years or more is that if you're going to end the relationship, you now have to stop thinking emotionally and start thinking financially. You will need to get prepared. To ensure your emotional survival, look into a good therapist too. Make sure you have one for you and any children involved. You'll need it, at least for a little while.

What Do You Know About Your Finances?

If your answer is anything but, "Oh, I handle all our finances; I know exactly where we are," then you have work to do. If you have been out of touch with your family finances for more than 5 years, don't even try to get caught up.

Get yourself to a CDFA™, ASAP! You can find one in your area by going to www.instituteDFA.com. Don't walk, RUN! And do it BEFORE you tell your spouse you want a divorce.

They'll help you do a little digging to get some information just in case it starts to disappear once you reveal your intentions. They'll also help you see what your financial life after divorce might look like.

Gather Documents

This is the one thing you can do to save yourself a ton of money in the divorce process. Anything you can gather before you meet with an attorney, a mediator, or a CDFA™ like myself, will reduce the amount you ultimately have to spend out of pocket.

- 3 years of tax returns with all supporting schedules and W-2s

- Last 3 months' statements on all investment accounts

- Last 3 months' statements for all bank accounts, checking and/or savings

- Most recent three statements from any employee retirement plan, pension, or deferred comp plan

- Most recent statement on any Employee Stock Option, Employee Stock Purchase Plan, or Restricted Stock accounts.

- Most recent mortgage statement

- Most recent pay stubs for each party

- Last 3 months' statements for any and all credit cards with balances

- Copies of most recent statements for any outstanding loans

- Policy statements or information on any and all Life Insurance, Annuities, or Cash Value Insurance

- Social Security Estimate statements for both parties. These are available at www.SSA.gov

- For any businesses owned, a full Profit and Loss Statement for current and previous years

- Most recent Insurance Policies for all autos owned that show VIN numbers. Write in current mileage on vehicle.

Get Organized

Now that you've gathered all the data, find a way to keep it all organized. It might be as simple as manila folders. I've seen some people create a 3-ring binder with tabs for each section. (I'm pretty sure these are the scrapbook people.) I'm a big fan of accordion files or those little portable file boxes with a handle that hold just enough to still carry around. The system you use is up to you but you'll need quick and easy access in a mobile format. Again, this will save you big bucks down the road.

Tell Your Spouse

This is the tough part. No matter how sure you are, no matter how kind you try to be, this is going to be one of the most difficult conversations you've ever had in your life. Unless you are in an abusive situation, for goodness sake, don't wimp out and send an email! Ugh! Suck it up and do it.

My ex was so gutless that he took me to a restaurant and told me not only that he wanted a divorce but dropped the bomb that he had been having an affair. HE TOLD ME IN A PUBLIC PLACE! Yeah, that's appropriate. Needless to say I got up and walked out. Don't do this to anyone that you once loved.

And after you've dropped the bomb, give the other person some space. They need time to process what you already have. If you have children, this is a great evening for them to go stay with Grandma and Grandpa or friends for the night. Respect that your spouse is going to go through a lot of emotion and the best place for you to be might be somewhere else.

CHAPTER 2 – GETTING STARTED

Ok, so you've finally jumped onto the divorce escalator and it's moving. There is no getting off. It's up to you if you want to plant yourself firmly, handle each move forward with grace and ease, or fight every step and end up thrown off into a heap at the top. Either way you'll end up divorced.

The first thing to tackle before you can even think straight is your emotions. No matter how much you've already processed or how long you've been thinking about doing it, divorce can be one of the most emotionally devastating things you'll ever go through.

Emotions

I'd like to share a blog I wrote for DivorcedMoms.com that later appeared on Huffington Post. You might relate.

White dress. Peach roses with baby's breath. Long veil. Happily, Ever After. That's the way it was supposed to be. I believed it. I wanted it. I needed it. Then he lied. Then he cheated. Then he left me.

He left me! I don't get left! If anyone's going to do any leaving, it's darn well going to be me! The betrayal after 16 years of marriage and 2 children was paralyzing. I felt as though my arms and legs had been brutally torn from my body and everything I knew of who I was disappeared in the instant he uttered the words, "I have something to tell you." I was lost, bobbing in the waters of what remained of my life, certain that drowning was imminent.

Then one day it started to change. About 15 days into my paralysis, the shift began. The sadness and loss gave way to unrelenting thoughts taking me back through the prior year revealing the numerous times his behavior didn't quite make sense.

The lies came into focus and I realized that I had not only been betrayed, but a fool as well. And I became angry. I'm not talking about "mad" angry; I'm talking "hunt-you-down-put-a-fork-in-your-face" angry!!! It was utterly consuming.

The anger was with me in the daytime, at my job, during the time with my kids, even in my dreams. I felt it in my chest as a gnawing heaviness that demanded to have a voice, demanded to be validated.

So instead of focusing on my own recovery and being strong for my kids, I found myself stalking his Facebook page, looking for evidence of his misery. I wanted him to be miserable. I found myself outside his apartment, fantasizing about putting a rock through his window and going Carrie Underwood on his car. I fantasized about meeting his girlfriend in a dark alley and going gangsta' on her ass!

And guess what he was doing. He was being happy with his new girlfriend in his new life. Who the heck did he think he was?! How dare he not be suffering like me!

Here I am 7 years later and realize what wasted energy that was. Do you know what I accomplished?

Here it is. Down and dirty.

1. I was consumed with anger every day and night and I felt miserable. He didn't.
2. I failed to plan for my future and my children's. Six months later I was nearly out of money.
3. My health deteriorated. I couldn't sleep, drank too much, and gained 15 lbs.
4. To stay angry meant I wasn't healing. I wasn't looking at MY role in the divorce.
5. My anger had me focused on the past instead of my present and my future.

Thankfully I had some very good friends that looked me in the eye and told me that it was time to move on. One friend in particular took my hand one day and said, "Sweetie, he's happy. How much longer are you going to give him the power to determine how you feel? Isn't it about time for you to take your life back and stop letting him be in control?"

Her words hit me like a ton of bricks and I decided then and there to take back control of my life. Things hadn't turned out the way I had planned. But so what? Now it was up to me to write the next chapter of my life. I planned a weekend alone to process my thoughts. I got quiet, listened to some good music, wrote in my journal and made a decision to take a step forward. I closed the book on my marriage and let it go. I wrote him a letter forgiving him and wishing him well. I didn't send it. It was for me, not him. He had already moved on.

The next morning when I opened my eyes, the sun was just a little brighter. The sky was just a little bluer. I even felt a little prettier. I had no idea what the next chapter

*would hold, but I was ready to put
my big girl panties on and find out.*

I share that because it's a vivid portrayal of
just how powerful – and destructive –
emotions can be if you don't allow yourself
time to process. One of the stupid mistakes
I made was not seeing a counselor. I really
needed it but I was going to be strong. I
don't need him. I'll be FINE. Yeah, right.

So step one, seriously consider seeing a
therapist or counselor even if only for a few
visits. If you just can't make that happen,
then be sure to ramp up your support
system. But beware. A support system is
NOT those friends that let you bitch and
moan about your ex and the divorce.
They're NOT the ones that think you should
get out and start dating right away. (That is
a horrible idea by the way.) They are the
friends that distract you with positive
activities like hiking, biking, yoga, shop-
ping, plays, etc.

One of the strange upsides to a divorce is
that for those with children, this may be the
first time in YEARS that you actually have
time for yourself. No kids, no spouse, no
expectations. It's really quite liberating.

Don't be surprised though when the first few times you're alone, without the kids or ex, you may very well have an emotional breakdown. That's a harsh moment when the changes hit pretty hard. I seem to remember my first night alone being accompanied by a bottle of vodka. Another stupid mistake; but necessary for me at the time.

A Word about "Fault"

You may be wondering exactly what does "no-fault" divorce mean? Listen up and hear this good because it's really, really important. No matter what your spouse has done, not done, said, not said, been or not been, unless they've been convicted of a crime, THE JUDGE DOESN'T CARE! The judge has heard over and over and over again about bad behavior leading up to divorces and in most states, it makes no difference whatsoever in the settlement of your case.

Once you're divorced, your ex is free to co-parent your children in any way they see fit, even if it's different than yours. He wants to have the kids sleep on the couch in his friend's basement so he can drink and play poker upstairs with his buddies – HE GETS

TO! Put very simply, it is not a crime to be an asshole.

This is the most difficult thing in the world for a mother to handle. We have zero control of what goes on with our children during the time they spend with their father. Yes, I'm gender stereotyping here but we women are the ones that typically obsess over this stuff. I will say though, I have seen some pretty atrocious behavior by women as well.

Rest assured that your children will come to their own conclusions in their own time. Let them do that. You don't have to say a word to them. You need to be their safe harbor. The place they can be comfortable and feel safe to be themselves.

For all you wonderful, conscientious dads that work with us in the best interest of the kids, bless you! Thank you for being mature and co-parenting with us to bring up these little humans in a loving, productive, cooperative way. Unfortunately I hear too many stories where that hasn't been the case.

Communication

The hardest part of this first phase for me was the communication with my ex. You start out trying really hard to be polite, but man the emotions are so close to the surface that they just fly out at the MOST inappropriate times. You're both dealing with the grief process, albeit in very different ways. Women will tend to be in sadness and mourning while men tend to be in anger. This is not usually a recipe for great communication.

It will help if you can both keep one thing in mind. The overriding emotion you are both feeling, whether or not you admit it, is FEAR. Will I be ok? Will I be broke? Will I become a bag lady? How will I earn money? Will I ever be able to retire? Will anyone ever love me again? Will I grow old and alone?

This stuff is real and totally overwhelming. If your spouse lashes out at you, try your best to see through what's actually being said and understand that all anger comes from fear. It will help you stay detached and not take it so personally.

Let's talk about email. I find that most couples, me included, try to communicate primarily via email to keep things less emotional and businesslike. It doesn't always work. My ex would send venomous diatribes via email; pages and pages of just nastiness. And I, of course, always felt the need to defend myself. Seriously? After 16 years of this dysfunctional communication did I really think I could get him to see the light now?

A great practice if this happens is to have someone else read your emails to your ex BEFORE you send them and take out ALL emotion and non-essential information. I finally realized that in these two-page rants from him, there was one very simple question and I would respond with one sentence answering it and pretend the rest didn't exist.

If you struggle with this, there are services out there for high-conflict divorce situations where they will edit your emails for you. Seriously. Check out OurFamilyWizard.com.

The best, most powerful three words I can offer you for the beginning, middle, end, and post-divorce phases is simple – LET IT GO! You'll be so much better for it. Look forward, not back. What's done is done. There's no longer a reason to try to fix it.

Decide on the Right Method

In this day and age, there are lots of ways to get a divorce, each with its own pros and cons. Which method you choose will depend largely on the relationship between you and your spouse. If you are afraid for your safety or the safety of your children for any reason at all, get a lawyer. Period.

If you believe that you and your spouse will be able to rationally sit down and discuss the details of your divorce and ultimately each want to be fair and honest, you might be able to do it yourself. In Arizona, and most states, it is incredibly easy to file divorce documents yourself at a minimal cost AS LONG AS YOU BOTH AGREE.

Fair warning here; just because you and your spouse are getting along today, doesn't mean it will always be this way. If you do your own documents, I highly recommend you have an attorney review them before you file. I made some really stupid mistakes when I did my own documents and it cost me over $12,000 in legal fees when I had to go back to court twice to fix them. You don't want to do that.

If your financial situation is a little more complex, perhaps there is a pension involved or one party is self-employed, or you own rental properties, then you might consider using a CDFA™ as a financial neutral to help you craft a fair settlement. Then have a legal document preparer do the rest. This is actually my favorite way to work. I've had one couple after another tell me that because we worked through their divorce settlement this way, they were able to remain friends. It's a respectful, honest way to go through the process and saves both parties having to pay legal fees.

If you are prepared to be in the same room with each other but are afraid it will just erupt into disagreements and fighting, then mediation may be right for you. This is a great way to have an independent third party there to help you negotiate items of disagreement. Again, it helps preserve the post-divorce relationship and keeps costs down.

Keep in mind that a mediator will NOT give you any advice on how to structure your settlement. If your financial situation is complex at all, bring in a neutral CDFA™ to help you craft the smartest settlement possible.

I started using this team approach a couple of years into my practice and it was so successful that I trademarked it as MediationPlus™ and now market it nationally with qualified practitioners listed on the website: www.MediationPlus.expert.

One step up from this model is Collaborative Divorce. This is ideal for high net worth, complex situations where privacy is a concern. It's a team model where each party has their own representative attorney, there is a financial neutral, and at least one therapist to represent the children and their needs. Sometimes a therapist/coach is also brought on for each client to help them navigate the process.

As you can see, with so many people involved it's not cheap. But for the couples that use it, it's a lot cheaper than going to court. The motivation to settle is also high because if the process fails, all of the professionals are conflicted out and the couple has to start from scratch with new attorneys. Yikes.

Lastly, if one or both parties can't manage to cooperate at any level and seem determined to go to war, then hiring attorneys may be your only option. Say goodbye to about $10,000 each at a minimum. Even in a litigation situation, having a financial expert on your team will be crucial.

Road Maps

Let's take each method and give you an idea of how it works.

<u>Do It Yourself</u>

In most states the process is pretty similar and has about four steps or so.

1. One party files the initial petition and is now the "petitioner." This is really just a notice to the state that you intend to divorce. It can include your proposed settlement but doesn't have to. It will usually include a list of all assets and debts, kids, etc.

2. The other party has to "accept service" and becomes the "respondent." This happens either voluntarily by signing a form in front of the clerk of the court or a notary, or by being served by a process server: the method most often portrayed in movies.

3. The respondent has 20 days or so to file a formal response if they

disagree with the proposed settlement in the petition. In a do it yourself, usually the petition will just say "pending agreements" so there won't be a need for a response.

4. After the mandatory waiting period that is different by state (see Appendix D) you both sign in front of a notary and file your Consent Decree. Your state might call it something else. The Consent Decree contains all your agreements and a parenting plan if you have minor children.

5. The judge will review and sign your decree and send you each a copy. This can take one week to 3 months depending on how back-logged your courts are.

6. Once you receive the signed copy, you're officially divorced.

Mediation or MediationPlus™

The process will be almost the same as do-it-yourself except that between steps one and four, you will have meetings with your mediator and/or CDFA™ to work out the details of your settlement. One difference is sometimes nothing is filed until after the settlement agreement is reached and another major difference is usually the mediator or someone on their staff will be preparing all of your documents.

Collaborative Divorce

Collaborative Divorce can actually take many forms these days. There is the formal process endorsed by the International Academy of Collaborative Practitioners (IACP), but more and more professionals are coming up with their own modified versions. Here are a few key bullet points to keep in mind:

- The process is private
- Each party has an attorney and sometimes a therapist involved
- All parties agree to work toward full settlement without litigation
- If the process fails, ALL professionals are conflicted out from representing the parties and they would need to start over with new attorneys.

For more information on the Collaborative model and to find practitioners in your area go to http://www.collaborativepractice.com.

<u>Attorney Only</u>

If you're not fortunate enough to be in a situation where you can use one of the previously mentioned methods and are going to be forced to get an attorney, be sure to interview a few and ask questions to determine if they are the right attorney for you. Here's a sampling of questions that will help:

1. <u>"What percentage of your cases typically go to trial?"</u>

   If the answer to this is more than 20%, BEWARE! That would indicate an overly litigious attorney who doesn't really want you and your spouse to settle but is more interested in racking up billable hours.

2. <u>"Will you or someone in your office be helping me prepare an accurate Financial Affidavit?"</u>

   They better answer yes. The financial affidavit will form the basis of all your settlement discussions, child support, and any claim for maintenance. Are you sure your budget is accurate? Have you forgotten any expenses that you aren't used to paying? Is your budget supposed to reflect current expenses or post-divorce expenses?

3. <u>"Will you be reviewing my spouse's Financial Affidavit for accuracy?"</u>

I find that very few attorneys will examine your spouse's affidavit for errors. At the very least, tax withholding is almost always still being calculated as "Married" when it should be "Single." Often I see mistakes in calculating Social Security and I also see many expenses being double-counted. If no one is looking for these things, it could seriously hurt your case.

4. <u>If you have been a homemaker: "How soon will I be expected to be back at work and what will be the earning expectation?"</u>

This is a major, major deal. If you've been a stay-at-home parent for 5 years or more, your skills are outdated no matter what your background is. Be aware that in some states, you will be expected to be self-supporting very quickly unless you are disabled in some way. You'll need a plan. If an attorney tries to tell you that you may get maintenance for more than 5 years, he/she is likely telling you what you want to hear and looking forward to their nice fat case file when you let them fight for an unrealistic settlement.

There are exceptions to this. In states like California, New York, New Jersey, and Illinois, the maintenance climate is different and much longer-term awards are still seen. But these are fewer and fewer.

5. **"Will my spouse and I have an opportunity to negotiate a settlement?"**

I find that most attorneys just shuttle written offers back and forth between you and your spouse's attorney without offering you a settlement negotiation meeting. Why? Because they get to bill more for doing all the document write-ups and responses. Imagine how productive it would be if you both could meet in a room with your attorneys and actually speak to each other on each point. Ask if your attorney is willing to do this.

6. <u>"Is it ok if I add a Divorce Financial Planner to the team to help me be better prepared for what kind of settlement I should try to get?"</u>

Again, if the answer to this is anything but "yes," BEWARE. Why would an attorney not want you to have all the information you need? Don't be surprised if your attorney doesn't know anything about Certified Divorce Financial Analysts, CDFAs™ and their work. In Arizona, attorneys call in forensic accountants and don't realize that a CDFA™ has nearly the same skill set.

Attorneys are very protective of their billable hours and aren't really interested in delving into the intricacies of the financials of your case. They also are NOT financial specialists and won't really want to do anything other than opt for a 50/50 split on everything which is RARELY the best thing for any couple. But there is an exception to this. If you find a family law attorney who is ALSO a CPA or CDFA™, now you have a winner. IF not, a CDFA™

can save the two of you thousands of dollars in both taxes and attorney fees.

7. "I think my spouse may be hiding assets. How will you be sure we know about everything?"

   They should respond to this with assurances that they will be going over several years of tax returns and bank statements to look for any anomalies. However, in order to really know for sure if assets are being hidden or diverted, a forensic accountant or CDFA™ is necessary to do the detailed work.

8. "My spouse owns a business and says it's not worth anything but we live on over $100,000 per year. How will we know the true value of the business and how will the judge know his true income?"

   They should answer that a formal business valuation will be ordered to establish a fair market value of the business. To determine an accurate assessment of annual income, a lifestyle analysis should be done. I've never known an attorney to do these in-house. They should be bringing in a CDFA™ or forensic accountant to establish the basis for an annual income claim.

9. <u>"I want to keep the house but don't have enough equity to refinance. What are my options?"</u>

In my experience, most attorneys will say you have two options: either refinance the home or sell. Now some will say you can keep the house as long as your spouse will allow you to keep their name on the mortgage. I've never heard them suggest other options. Here are a few that a CDFA™ can help you explore:

a. Continue to own the house jointly for a period of years, usually 3-5, at which point you would either sell or refinance and split the proceeds.

b. Continue to own the house jointly for a period of years, usually 3-5, but the spouse not living there would receive other assets in lieu of his/her share of the equity. To protect their credit, a clause can be written in that you must provide proof of mortgage payment each month and if at any point the mortgage is more than 30 days past due, the house must be sold.

c. Continue to own the house jointly and rent it out. A CDFA™ can help with the terms of such an arrangement.

10. "The only assets we have are 401(k) accounts but I need money for a down payment on a house. How can I get cash?"

As part of your divorce settlement, if 401(k) assets are transferred to the non-participating spouse via QDRO, Qualified Domestic Relations Order, they have ONE opportunity to remove cash with no penalties. The amount would be taxed as ordinary income but there would be no early withdrawal penalty. This can be a great way to get cash to both parties.

CHAPTER 3 - PROPERTY

One of the first things you'll probably start to think about is who gets what. It's inevitable. There can be some strange emotions tied to our "stuff." (BTW, I LOVE George Carlin! If you've never seen his routine on "stuff," find it on YouTube for a good belly laugh!)

If you were the one to decorate your home, you may feel like it is a reflection of you and want to take all of it with you. On the other hand, you might feel like all your stuff is contaminated by dysfunctional marriage juju and you never want to see it again.

When I left my marital home, I only took a couple of things. I really wanted a clean, fresh start. Then, 30 days later when his new girlfriend was threatened by my belongings, I came home one day to find every decorator item I had ever purchased stacked up on the sidewalk outside the door of my new home. Piled up coffee tables, artwork, knick-knacks, dining table and chairs, even a set of bookcases that had belonged to HIS mother greeted me like a monument to our messed up lives. I entered the house through the garage, closed the door, and went on with my night until I was ready to decide how to deal with it.

Let's get down to business. Here's my philosophy. All the crap in your house – just work it out. Make sure the person who leaves takes what they need or enough cash to get what they need. And YES, this should come out of marital funds. Come on people. You built the marriage together, make sure you each have what you need to get started apart. If neither of you want the stuff, have a giant yard sale and split the proceeds.

I actually had one of those quickie, "too young, doesn't count," marriages. I got married a week before my 19th birthday to a sailor who was going to take me to exotic places and away from my little hometown. We were technically married about 3 years but only physically together for less than 18 months. We ended it amicably. We actually sat down with clipboards – and beer. We had ourselves a little party and went through all our stuff and played "Who Gets What."

When we started realizing that all we had was a bunch of junk, we turned it into a comedy routine. "Oh no, baby, I REALLY think you need to take this. No REALLY! I WANT you to have it!" We drank, laughed, cried, but ultimately got through it fine. Yes, I realize this isn't always possible but it is actually one of the best memories I have of that brief marriage. I hardly ever speak of it anymore; feels like it wasn't even my life.

Community Property or Equitable Division

Ok, so let's say you're NOT so amicable. Well, then the first thing you need to do is figure out if your state is a Community Property state or an Equitable Division state. (See Appendix D)

If you live in a Community Property state, then the courts will pretty much divide all your assets and debts to result in a 50/50 split. The good news is that if you and your spouse agree, you can do anything you want as long as it's basically fair.

In an Equitable Division state, there can be some grey areas that result in uneven property awards. For instance, let's say a husband worked his wife through medical school, stayed home with the kids for 20 years and is now divorcing his heart-surgeon wife. The judge could rule that he deserves to be compensated for the sacrifice of his own earning potential and he could get more than half of their accumulated property.

This is just an example. Again though, through mediation, a couple can work towards agreement and not get too hung up on the specifics of the law.

I take some heat from attorneys when I say things like that because they see a lot of cases where one spouse is abusive, controlling, dealing with mental disorders, etc. Let me be clear. If ANY of these apply to you, then you need an attorney and you'll need to get educated on your state's laws. That's not the purpose of this book.

Separate vs Marital

Moving on to the next task – is the property to be split or does it belong only to one spouse? How do we know? Each state has some different laws on separate property but most of them are similar. Bottom line – if you owned something before the marriage and still do, it's yours alone. If you purchased or acquired it during the marriage, it's marital and gets split.

The exception to that rule is inheritance. If you inherit money or property – AS LONG AS YOU KEEP IT IN YOUR NAME ALONE – it is your separate property. In some states like California, even if you didn't keep it in your name alone but you can trace the value of the inheritance clearly, they'll still find it to be separate property.

Let's say you inherit $50,000 and you just plop it into your joint bank account where it pays bills, home remodeling, kid camps, etc. over the next 10 years and is pretty much gone. My experience is that MOST courts will find that it's a "presumptive gift to the marriage" and no longer separate property.

A real grey area exists around student loans. If you come into the marriage with student loans, they're yours. BUT if you take them out during the marriage and your resulting education provides you with a significantly higher earning capacity than your spouse, they can still be determined to be separate property.

Keep in mind too that student loans cannot be split. Not officially anyway. What I've had to set up is a Property Settlement Note where the non-student spouse pays half the payment each month to the other spouse who then pays the full loan payment. There is no splitting or refinancing of a student loan into someone else's name.

The critical question to ask is did, or will, both parties benefit from this asset or debt. If you both benefited, it needs to be split fairly.

Probably the biggest mistake I see couples, and attorneys for that matter, make when they are negotiating their settlement is thinking of each asset and debt individually. Maybe there is a $100k savings account and a rental property worth $100k. Depending on the tax status of the rental, these two assets might offset each other so that one person can keep the rental and the other the cash.

I see a lot of people thinking if the rental has $100k in equity, then the one that wants to keep it HAS to refinance and pay out half the equity to the other party. No! Indeed, you may have to refinance but you also could offset the asset with something else. Maybe it makes the most sense to give $58,823 in 401k assets instead. ($50k grossed up for 15% taxes)

I REALLY encourage people to get creative with their settlements. I'm a firm believer that EVERY divorce has a win/win situation just waiting to be flushed out. That's why I love my work so much. It's pretty rewarding to see emotional, divorcing couples get all excited because their settlement is working out so much better than they expected.

Another issue with separate property that varies from state to state is whether or not the growth on that separate property is marital or separate. (See Appendix D for your state.)

For example, in Arizona the growth on separate property is also separate property. So, let's say Debbie has a 401k worth $50,000 at the time she gets married and then continues to work and contribute to that plan for another 15 years until the time of her divorce when it's worth $375,000. How much is separate property? Yikes. There's a math problem huh?

This is the type of service that a CDFA™ or Financial Forensic can offer. The fact of the matter is you have to separate out the original balance from the new contributions and then calculate the compounding growth on the original balance only for each period of returns to get the separate amount. It's a heck of an excel spreadsheet, let me tell you.

The result is that about $175,000 of that 401k is actually separate property. And guess what? If you don't bring that up to an attorney, they may never ask and you may never get credit for that fact. Remember, attorneys and judges are NOT financial people.

Date of Separation

The last detail on property involves knowing the correct split date. As usual, this also varies by state. In Arizona, everything is based on the date of petition. Some states use a date of separation, and some states use an actual date of decree. A little googling will answer that question.

Once again, if a couple is cooperative, they can choose the date that makes sense. I find many couples just choose either the last day of a month or calendar year to make taxes and everything else cleaner. The date you choose does matter though because that's the date that everything is no longer "ours" but instead, "his" or "hers." From that point forward, each party is responsible for their own assets, debts, expenses, etc.

And now that you're educated on property settlements, I feel it only appropriate to share with you my . . .

TOP 3 STUPID MISTAKES MADE IN DIVORCE SETTLEMENTS

Take these to heart. Let me help you NOT be a dummy.

I see a few things over and over again when it comes to divorce settlements that were agreed to (and sometimes even ordered by a judge) where the people come to me after the fact confused and bewildered. I read through their decree and just shake my head. Please, please, please – DON'T make these mistakes!

#3 – The settlement doesn't take taxes into effect – AT ALL!

For heaven's sake people, really? We all know that Uncle Sam will dive into our pockets at every opportunity. How could you possibly agree to a settlement without knowing the tax implications? Many people have been stunned to find out that the tax burden on their half of the marital assets is significantly higher than their spouse's making their "half" of the assets worth significantly less than they thought. And DON'T expect your attorney to do this. Attorneys are NOT accountants or financial advisors and a lot of them won't bother to warn you about taxes. Buyer beware.

#2 – Pensions are split 50/50 but no one knows what that really means.

Over and over and over I see divorce decrees that order pensions split 50/50 but no one has any idea what will actually happen. When does the non-employee spouse start collecting? Is there an option to take a lump sum? Will there be a cost of living increase each year? What if the employee spouse dies? Will it keep paying? When I ask these questions, no one has ANY IDEA what the answers are? Really? How can you possibly agree to a settlement where this piece is crucial to your retirement without knowing these details? Again, do not expect attorneys or mediators to be of much help here.

#1 – Drum Roll – The biggest stupid mistake I see is keeping a house you can't afford.

Women especially tend to be emotionally tied to the family home and often insist on staying. Did they do a budget? Nope. Did they meet with a financial planner? Nope. Then one or two years down the road they run out of cash and realize that they can't sell a window to put food on the table. They can't refinance because now they don't have enough income and they realize they have no choice but to sell. The selling costs are about 8% of the sale – all of which WOULD have been split 50/50 with the ex if they had sold as part of the divorce. Stupid, stupid, stupid.

So listen, I know "stupid" is not a very nice word and probably ignorance is more accurate. But please, realize what you DON'T know and bring in the right experts for your divorce to make sure that you are SMART and make the best decisions you can with ALL the information. Don't go this alone. As we say at Smarter Divorce Solutions, "You only have one chance to get it right!"

CHAPTER 4 –
RETIREMENT
ACCOUNTS

There's a good chance that retirement accounts are the largest assets you have accumulated. When people aren't looking, a 401(k) or pension can grow to a value of a million dollars or more pretty quickly. First, let's list the different kinds of accounts we're talking about:

401(k)
403(b)
457 Plans
Traditional IRA
SEP IRA
Roth IRA
Simple IRA
Keogh
SARSEP Plans

Profit Sharing Plans

Money Purchase Plans

ESOP – Employee Stock Ownership Plans (not to be confused with ESPP, Employee Stock Purchase Plans)

409A Nonqualified Deferred Compensation Plans

Overwhelmed yet? But wait. Guess what else? Just to keep you confused, all of these have different taxation. Some are defined benefit and some are defined contribution. And you're thinking, "What the heck does that mean?" I KNOW. How are you supposed to know all this stuff?

You're not. That's why you bring in someone who does. But let me give you some basics. You can also find good information on the IRS Website at http://www.irs.gov/Retirement-Plans/Plan-Sponsor/Types-of-Retirement-Plans-1.

Defined Contribution Plans

This is a fancy name for all plans where you know how much you're putting in, but you don't really know how much you'll have when you go to take it out. These are the most common today. This is your 401(k), all IRA accounts, Profit Sharing and Money Purchase Plans. (Those last two you hardly ever see by the way, unless you are highly compensated like a doctor, movie star or Michael Jordan.)

Within defined contribution plans, you can have two types – pre-tax or tax deferred and post-tax or Roth. I can hear the financial advisors out there going "Hold on. It's not that simple." Yeah, yeah, stay with me.

Here are a few more definitions:

Tax-deferred – This is when you invest money and it grows for a long time and you don't pay taxes on it until you take it out, usually in retirement after you are at least 59 ½-years-old.

Now, the money you put in MIGHT be pre-tax, if you qualify. Check with your accountant or advisor. If it is, that's a great deal as it reduces your current income tax. But you still have to pay taxes on that money when you take it out. The thought is that you will be at a lower tax rate in retirement than you are now. Be careful though. We currently have the lowest income tax rates the U.S. has seen in over 100 years matched with the highest debt levels. There's a good chance you may have to pay MORE taxes when you are in retirement.

Roth – Some companies now give you the option to designate up to half of your 401(k) contributions as Roth. Roth is a beautiful word. You should know it, love it, and use it. As a financial advisor, few things make my heart go pitter-pat as much as a Roth account.

When you put money into a Roth, whether 401(k) or IRA, you pay taxes on that contribution now, at the LOWEST RATES IN 100 YEARS, and you will NEVER PAY TAXES ON ANY OF IT AGAIN! Yes, I'm serious. With the current government debt levels, I'm convinced that this vehicle will eventually go away when the government figures out how much it's costing them so milk it for all it's worth after you've con-firmed with your advisor that it makes sense for your individual situation.

Everyone can contribute to a Roth 401(k) if your company offers it but to contribute to a Roth IRA, you must be below the income limits. Check the current year income limits on the IRS website and if your adjusted gross income is below those numbers, you would most likely be served very well by opening a Roth. Check with your advisor for sure. If not, don't despair, there's an answer for you too.

Backdoor Roth – Thanks to legislation that passed in 2010, there are currently no income limits on converting Traditional IRA dollars to a Roth IRA. That means that you can put money into an IRA, it may or may not be deductible depending on your income and other retirement plan availability, then do an immediate conversion to your Roth IRA. If the original contribution was deductible, you will go ahead and pay the taxes on it and BAM; you just funded your Roth. If you are interested in this, check with your advisor soon because we're all pretty sure that loophole will close eventually.

But I digress. So any defined contribution plan that was accumulated during the marriage is owned 50/50. Doesn't matter whose name is on it. Doesn't matter that only one person earned any money. It belongs to both of you. Period.

Defined Benefit Plans (Pensions)

These are the reverse of the Defined Contribution Plans. You don't know exactly how much you will ultimately contribute, a great deal of which is contributed by your employer, but you know exactly how much you will receive in a monthly payment upon a certain retirement age. Usually you will have a full-retirement age, an early-retirement age with a lower monthly payment, and maybe even a delayed-retirement age with a higher monthly payment. In all cases, the payments are made via an annuity with several different payout options that allow for beneficiary designations, survivor benefits, etc.

Pensions used to be commonly offered retirement plans and now are almost entirely limited to government employees or the very high-level executives of large publicly traded companies. Pensions made sense for employers when employees used to stay at the same company for 30+ years but today, with the average American having more than 10 different employers in their lifetime, not so much.

Also the political trend has been to shift the retirement burden from the companies to the individual. We could talk about why but that would go down this really gnarly political path and half of my readers would decide they didn't like me anymore. It would just generally be a bad idea.

There is one thing to remember about a pension over everything when it comes to divorce. If you learn nothing else from this chapter, learn this and learn it well. THE VALUE OF THE PENSION ON THE STATEMENT IS **NOT THE TRUE VALUE.** It's worth more. A LOT more.

I am stunned when I discover yet another Family Law Attorney that doesn't know this. A current pension statement only shows the sum of the dollars contributed to date. To actually value that pension, you need a very complex valuation done. It is always much more than what the statement says.

No one likes math so I won't go into the calculation but here's the basic concept. The value of the pension is how much money would have to be invested today to provide that stream of income for life at age 65, or whatever the retirement age is. So you have to factor in inflation, earnings, more con-tributions, etc.

Contributions made after date of separation don't contribute to the marital portion so any growth in that pension post-divorce belongs to the person earning it.

Valuation is huge, but there's more to worry about; especially if the earner is a police officer or firefighter. There are some serious pitfalls to know. For example, in Arizona, let's say a police officer assigns 50% of his pension to his wife in a divorce. Then, after only 5 years of collecting, he dies. Well, guess what? Her pension will only continue paying as long as his actual dollars contributed are available. This usually provides for less than 10 years of payments.

I recently had a case where he had already been collecting his pension for 6 years and his original contributions were fully depleted. In this case, the minute he passes, the wife's share of the pension ends. AND the pension will NOT allow him to list an ex-wife as a beneficiary. Oh, and to make matters worse, he has high blood pressure and sleep apnea and is practically uninsurable for a life insurance policy to secure maintenance. Wow. What a mess huh?

So, be SURE someone is checking into all the subtleties of any pension. There can be a LOT of issues lurking there that could seriously impact your future.

Retirement planning is probably the most significant casualty of divorce for couples 45-65. That retirement plan that was adequate for a couple is likely to be woefully underfunded when broken into two. Before you agree to ANY kind of settlement, make sure you understand what your future will look like and how you will need to adjust your expectations.

Qualified Domestic Relations Order (QDRO)

To divide most of these retirement plans, with the exception of IRA accounts, you will need to have a QDRO prepared. This is an additional legal document that gets certified by the judge stating the exact split of any retirement account.

Beware. The cost of QDRO preparation ranges from $400 to as much as $3,000. There is NO REASON a QDRO should cost $3,000. They're just not that difficult to do, no matter what your attorney might tell you. My firm facilitates QDROs at a reasonable flat fee and we're the best deal in town. Chances are there's someone local who will do the same for you.

A QDRO doesn't get prepared until ALL details of your settlement are finalized and typically can't be filed with the court until AFTER your decree has been entered.

Retirement Plan Option for Cash

As I mentioned previously, a little know option for anyone receiving retirement funds from a spouse in divorce via a QDRO is that you have ONE opportunity to withdraw cash from that plan before age 59 ½ with NO PENALTY. If it's a tax deferred plan, you will have to pay taxes on the amount withdrawn as ordinary income but will not have to pay the 10% penalty. This could be very helpful if you need cash for a house down-payment. You can only do this once so be sure to plan well up front.

The other thing you can do with a retirement plan is file for 72t early retirement and take funds out earlier than age 59 ½ with no penalty. 72t is the code in the IRS that provides for this. You can do this at any age. It basically will dictate an annuity amount that you will then be OBLIGATED to take out annually for at least 5 years based on one of three formulas. I encourage you to check with your financial advisor on all the details. More detailed information is available at www.irs.gov.

CHAPTER 5 - ALIMONY (Spousal Maintenance)

Of all the financial issues in divorce, this is the most hotly contested, most misunderstood, and most fought over in nearly every case. To complicate things further, the various state laws around alimony (some states call it alimony and some call it maintenance. I'll use "alimony" from this point forward but know that they are the same) are changing dramatically and quickly to reflect our changing cultural norms.

History

In the 1970's and 1980's when no-fault divorce was adopted in most states, marriage was viewed as a contract for life and when that contract was broken the parties were entitled to be "made whole" as much as possible. At that time, women serving as homemakers and mothers were very, very common. It was pretty normal for them to award lifetime maintenance to homemakers who had been married 10 years or more. The thought process was that the marriage contract had promised her a lifetime of support in exchange for the management of the home and the raising of the children.

According to the Bureau of Labor Statistics, the contribution to family earnings of women in the workforce has gone from 30.7% in 1990 to 37.3% in 2014. Obviously there are still plenty of full-time home-makers out there, both men and women. Are they vulnerable? Well, that depends on what state they live in. Seriously. Believe it or not, New York just adopted no-fault divorce in 2010. They are still one of the few states where lifetime maintenance awards are common.

Everywhere else in the US, the trend is toward the elimination of lifetime alimony in all but a few special situations which include disability of a party or adult chil-dren that require full-time care. Most states have revised their statutes deeming mainte-nance awards to be for "rehabilitative" purposes only and only for a period of time to allow the recipient to become "self-sufficient."

Well, what the heck does that mean? In Arizona each judge gets to decide exactly how much income is required to be "self-sufficient." In one of my cases, the couple had been living on $450,000 per year for the previous 10 years. They had been married for 32 years and the wife had never worked outside the home. The judge in her case deemed that she should have total income of $70,000 a year for 3 years, $50,000 for year 4 and $35,000 for year five at which point maintenance would end. And her ex-husband would go on earning $450,000 per year for another 15 years. Yes, seriously.

Only a handful of states still refer to the marital standard of living in their alimony statutes. A few of the notable ones are California, Illinois, New York, and New Jersey. There may be others but you need to find out what the environment in your state is before you start assuming you know what you'll get.

The reality in this day and age is that if you choose to be a stay-at-home parent, you are EXTREMELY vulnerable in a divorce situation. I have children in their early 20's and I've made sure they understand this fact. Times are changing.

Determining Factors

Several things are taken into consideration if the court is to award alimony. As usual, they differ by state but here's a pretty comprehensive list:

- Length of marriage
- One party's need
- The other party's ability to pay
- The amount of marital property being awarded to each spouse
- The ages of the parties
- Needs of any dependents
- The health of both parties
- Sometimes "fault" depending on the state
- Contributions of one spouse to the profession of the other spouse
- Sometimes the marital standard of living (less and less)

Risks

Alimony comes with a bunch of risks that I make sure everyone is aware of. Almost all alimony is modifiable. That means that with a significant change in circumstances, either party can go back to court and request that it be changed. If either the payor or recipient should become disabled, things could change dramatically overnight.

Now in a mediation, a couple could agree to make alimony NON-modifiable but that comes with risks too. If the payor can't work anymore, how are they supposed to make those payments and vice versa? There is now a disability insurance policy to secure maintenance and/or college expenses in a divorce that allows a potential solution.

Another risk is that the payor decides to be deliberately under-employed to reduce earnings and convince the court they should pay less. Judges are typically pretty unforgiving here but it has been done. Or in an extreme case, the payor decides to go off the grid, disappears to some island in the Caribbean, and is never heard from again. Good luck collecting your money.

The main thing I don't like about typical alimony is that the two spouses continue to be tied to each other. One party has to write that check each month and the other party can't pay the bills until they do. Leaves a LOT of room for deliberate manipulation as a subtle little revenge tactic that just isn't healthy.

No one likes having to pay maintenance and most will think it's just not fair, except of course, the recipient. The recipient typically feels they sacrificed for the marriage and are owed reimbursement for that sacrifice. Ultimately I think both parties are entitled to have the best chance of success in their next phase of life. If that means one of them needs to go back to school and reinvent themself to be able to earn a reasonable income, then it makes sense to set up a situation where both parties can be successful.

Lastly, keep in mind that alimony ends if the recipient remarries. I've heard over and over from payors that want to put in a clause that says it ends if the recipient cohabitates with someone too. In most states, that isn't going to happen. However, I have heard that a few states actually allow this stipulation! I joke with my payors that if they really don't want to keep paying, they need to find their wives a nice rich new boyfriend. Gives them a chuckle.

Options

Given the risks above, what other options are available? A CDFA™ can help you calculate a present-value buyout of all or part of the alimony so that you get cash up front instead. This is often a really good option when the payor just can't get their mind around the numbers.

Other options could include agreements to continue to own the primary home together, sharing in the mortgage payments for a period of years to reduce the expenses of the lower-wage earner. Then when the house is sold, they can split the profits and at least the money going to the house felt like an investment instead of just lost money.

Taxation

Typically alimony is tax deductible to the payor and taxable to the recipient. This is usually advantageous to both parties if the payor is in a higher tax bracket. It is another area where some creativity can be employed to save both parties money in the long run. It's too complicated to detail here. I'll just leave it that you should get some good analysis of different options by a CDFA™ or accountant who's well versed.

Beware of Recapture

*"If your **alimony** payments decrease or end during the first 3 calendar years, you may be subject to the **recapture rule**. If you are subject to this **rule**, you have to include in income in the third year part of the **alimony** payments you previously deducted." – IRS Publication 17, chapter 18. Alimony*

Bottom line, the IRS wants its money. So if alimony drops in the first 3 years, the IRS says it's really a veiled property settlement and should not have been tax deductible. The payor will have to pay them back at the higher tax rate and the recipient will get all their paid tax back. Good to keep in mind!

Also, make sure alimony doesn't stop within 6 months of a child turning 18 or you're also vulnerable to an IRS audit determining that your alimony was actually veiled child support and must be claimed as income by the payor. See IRS Publication 17, chapter 18.1 for more information.

As you can see there are several rules you need to know about alimony to make sure it continues to qualify as maintenance. Just because a payment is called alimony doesn't mean the IRS will agree with you. The IRS set out some rules in 1984 to try to clear up the confusion. Here are the criteria for a payment to qualify as alimony:

- The payment must be in cash
- The payments must be required by the decree or settlement agreement
- The decree cannot state that the payments are not spousal support
- The parties cannot be members of the same household when the payments are made
- The payments cannot qualify as child support as defined by the Internal Revenue Code
- The payments must cease upon the death of the recipient
- The spouses may not file a joint tax return

So, don't ever agree to buy your kids a new bed instead of paying your support. The IRS would frown heavily on that. And don't offer to do your ex's yardwork as a swap.

There is ONE exception to this. If your decree states that part of your alimony will be making a mortgage payment on your ex's behalf, then that payment IS considered alimony and tax deductible as long as your name is NOT on the title of the house. If your name is still on the title and you own it jointly then only half of the payment can be considered spousal maintenance.

CHAPTER 6 – CHILD SUPPORT

For anyone with minor children at the time of the divorce, unless you have similar incomes and agree to a substantially equal parenting time arrangement, one of you will likely be paying some level of child support.

Unlike alimony, almost every state has a very specific child support calculator that will determine the amount to be paid. It will take into consideration the earnings of both parents, any childcare expenses being paid, any cost of health insurance being provided by one parent, as well as the time the child(ren) will be spending with each parent to determine the amount.

Just as there have been recent trends in alimony, there are also trends in child support. Deadbeat parents are no longer tolerated and payors of child support can easily end up in jail if they fail to meet their obligations. Most states require employers to withhold child support directly from a payor's paycheck and send the payments to a state clearinghouse on their behalf.

In Arizona, if a child support payment is not made through the clearinghouse, it's deemed not to have been made at all. In other words, if dad gets laid off and gives mom a check directly since his employer won't be withholding, the state finds that to be a "gift" and he is now in arrears on his payments. He was correct to make out a check himself, but should have sent it through the clearinghouse to avoid issues later.

What's Not Covered

When child support is calculated, you want to keep in mind that it's based on averages. So if your kids are into some expensive sport, go to private school, or require expensive medical care, tutoring, etc., you'll need to make sure that these things are addressed so they will continue. Don't make the mistake of settling for verbal agreements. You may not always be as cooperative as you are today and you want **everything** documented to avoid disputes later.

How Long

Child support will be payable until the child reaches age 18 or graduates from high school, whichever happens LAST. The only exception to this is if you have a special needs child that will remain a dependent. There are entire books written on this subject so if it applies to you, you'll need to do some additional research.

After the termination of the child support order, Family Courts do not require anyone to continue funding adult children and their expenses. However, if you put agreements into your decree about college expenses or health insurance coverage, etc., then that part of your decree could be enforceable in a civil court as a simple contract.

Enforcement of any of this is never easy but in my experience, just having the agreements in writing is largely effective in ensuring cooperation.

Other Expenses

A really effective solution for funding kids' expenses as they move through school and even into college is to continue to maintain a joint bank account for this purpose.

Start by doing an annual best-guess budget of the kids' expenses to include: camps, activity costs, clothes, school supplies, transportation costs, etc. Let's say the total comes up to $6,000 per year. That's $3,000 each or $250 per month. Each of you makes a monthly deposit into the account and all expenses are paid from that by whichever parent is "on duty" when the expense arises. Other couples will divide the total proportionately to their incomes so maybe it's a 60/40 split instead of 50/50. It seems to work really well with a little cooperation.

Changing Child Support

Child support is always modifiable with a change in circumstances. If either party's earnings change more than about 10%, or the children's expenses change significantly, recalculating child support is probably in order.

If a couple is cooperative with this, it can often be done without actually going back to court. Most jurisdictions have online calculators and self-service websites for a do-it-yourself filing as long as you are both in agreement.

Taxes

Child support is paid with after-tax dollars so the payor pays the taxes, not the recipient. There are no exceptions to this IRS rule.

CHAPTER 7 – DEBT & EXPENSES

Along with splitting assets comes splitting debts. This is sometimes more complicated because creditors don't have to honor what's in your decree. There is a ton of risk here that you need to be aware of. Let's talk about three kinds of debt:

1. Mortgage Debt
2. Consumer Debt
3. Student Loans

Mortgage Debt

With mortgage debt there is one simple rule. If your name is on the loan documents of your mortgage, then you are responsible for the debt. Period. A mortgage lender does not care if your divorce decree says that your husband got the house and will assume all the payments. If he stops making payments, it will be reported on your credit report too. If they begin foreclosure proceedings, it's also a foreclosure on your credit report. If they auction the house for less than you owe, they are coming after you for the difference.

Unfortunately I learned all of this the hard way. My ex got our primary home and one rental property. Both had been mortgaged in our names during our marriage. The agreement was that he would refinance the mortgages and have my name removed within 6 months. He didn't. The following year he let them go into foreclosure and my credit rating is still being affected 8 years later.

So, what's a couple to do? How do you protect yourself? Here is the basic agreement I recommend couples include in their decree to give them the best protection if the mortgage can't be refinanced at the time of the divorce. Your attorney will make sure that the wording is proper but here's the gist.

3 year agreement. Husband to have occupancy. Wife to discontinue equity participation.

Wife agrees to release any and all interest in the home as well any obligations. After 3 years, Husband is required to either refinance the mortgage or sell the property. (If it were more agreeable to the parties, this could also be whatever time works for the situation.) During that period, every month husband would provide wife proof of mortgage payment. Husband agrees that if, at any time, the mortgage payment is more than 30 days late, wife can either loan him the money to make the payment or it would be agreed that the house would be listed for sale. In order to preserve her right to enforce the agreements, wife would NOT sign a quitclaim deed until the refinance or sale. Husband would be free to sell or refinance earlier if able. As husband will be paying all expenses and maintenance, he is entitled to any and all appreciation if earned as well as deduction of all mortgage interest paid.

Since the wife doesn't get to force a sale until it is already 30 days past due on the mortgage and a sale is going to take some time, there is still the risk that late payments will impact her credit score but not as much as if she forces a short sale at the time of the divorce.

You could also alter this agreement so that the wife DOES continue to participate in the equity and they split the proceeds upon sale or refinance. A good deal more complicated and too much to go into here. Just know it can be done.

Keep in mind that with the more stringent lending standards after the great recession of 2007-2008, the fact that your name is still on a mortgage MAY impact your ability to get a new loan to buy your own home. At the time of writing, lending standards are easing and I have several mortgage lenders that will accept the decree and a history of payments made by the ex-spouse to NOT include that debt payment. In essence they look at you as a landlord with the ex as the tenant.

If you think you want to buy a home of your own, be sure to consult a mortgage lender for current underwriting qualification standards before you agree to let your name stay on a mortgage.

Consumer Debt

We're talking about credit cards, bank loans, personal loans, lines of credit, and car loans. As with mortgages, if your name is on the loan, they will come after you. So you need to make sure that any debts that you agree are no longer your responsibility get your name removed. The only way to do this is to refinance.

Now if you are on a credit card not as a joint tenant but as an additional signer, then they will remove your name from the account upon request. For any joint tenant debt, the accounts MUST BE CLOSED and the debt moved to a card or loan in the name of the person responsible or you will be very sorry if they quit making their payments.

A really good friend of mine was just forced to file bankruptcy to protect herself from her ex-husband's debts. He assumed several credit cards and a mortgage at the time of the divorce and no one gave her this information. A year later he quits paying – on everything. Guess who started calling her? Collectors – many of them several times a day. Then she got a notice that their old house was going into foreclosure: with her name on it. There will likely be a delinquency of over $100,000 if it's sold at auction and they will totally file suit for that amount. She could even be responsible for federal taxes on $50,000.

DON'T LET THIS HAPPEN TO YOU.

Student Loans

We talked earlier about Student Loans and how the courts look at them for division. Here's the crazy part. I've seen divorce decrees that say that the student loan debt will be split 50/50 but say absolutely nothing about HOW.

Guess what? You can't refinance student loan debt into someone else's name. You also can't split a loan after it's issued. So if you're only responsible for half the payment now, how does that work? Does your ex make half the payment directly to the lender? If so, how do you know he/she is doing it? And who is impacted if they don't? YOU.

Does the non-student make payments to you directly? If it's not spelled out in the decree and you're not on speaking terms with your ex, do you see how this is a recipe for disaster?

The right way to handle this is to either use other assets to equalize the debt or set up an enforceable property settlement note so the non-student spouse makes payments directly to the student loan payor.

Unfortunately this is the kind of stuff that lawyers and judges often don't understand. It's not their fault. It's just not their specialty. Be sure you seek out the right experts to make sure you understand your risks and options.

CHAPTER 8 - INSURANCE

Divorce has several areas of concern that may require specific insurance policies for protection. The most obvious are alimony and child support, but there are others. This is a time when a review of all of your existing policies needs to happen.

Basics

Before we move on, let's get familiar with some of the basic terminology. Every insurance policy has three people involved: the owner, the insured, and the beneficiary.

The owner of the policy is the one that can make changes, the insured is the person whose life is being insured, and the beneficiary is the person who will receive money if the insured dies.

Any one of the three people can pay the premiums but only the owner can change the beneficiary or make adjustments to the policy. While there are three roles, one person can easily hold two of the roles. The owner might be the insured, or the beneficiary or a completely different third party.

Life Insurance

If you are going to be the recipient of either child support or alimony, what will happen if the payor dies prematurely? Do you know? You certainly better.

If you're counting on child support to be able to pay the bills, then a life insurance policy on the payor is imperative. It's not the only option but certainly the most common.

Other solutions involve the payor establishing a trust account that would continue to make payments to you after his death. This is more expensive to set up and manage but if there are plenty of assets to cover the obligation, it can make a lot of sense. The same type of trust can be established to continue paying your alimony as a claim against the estate of the payor.

This won't help you in the case of disability though. There is an insurance company that is now specializing in creative policies; disability policies to secure alimony, child support, even college costs that someone has agreed to pay. If the insured doesn't have a super-dangerous job, the premiums aren't even that much.

A note about life insurance: if a policy is to be taken out to cover alimony or child support, then one of two things needs to happen. Either the beneficiary is listed as **the irrevocable** beneficiary, meaning it can't be changed, or the beneficiary is also the owner of the policy. That way there is no risk of manipulation.

We've all heard stories of some jerk getting remarried and changing the beneficiary to his new wife just because he can. If this actually happens, it would be a long, lengthy, expensive, court battle to get your money and you might not win.

Health Insurance

Before passage of the Affordable Care Act, this was a really big deal. There were thousands of people that if they didn't have access to employer provided insurance, they simply couldn't get insurance at all. For this population, the Affordable Care Act was a huge victory.

We can debate the other aspects of the changes but that would lead to a real messy debate so, let's just focus on this. No one needs to be that concerned anymore with losing health insurance coverage from an employer. Yes your own policy will cost more than you were paying before but it won't likely be that different. It just becomes an import budget item when negotiating maintenance or child support.

So, if you will be losing your coverage after your divorce, be sure to meet with a health insurance agent to see what it's going to cost you. Divorce is a qualifying event that will allow you to enroll at any time of the year when you lose your coverage.

Those are the two biggies. Of course you want to make sure to update your auto and homeowner's or renter's insurance but this is usually done in a quick phone call to the agent. No big deal.

CHAPTER 9 – SOCIAL SECURITY

Social Security always seems to be a bit of a mystery to everyone. You know there's something you need to know but you're not sure what; something about 10 years, right? Ok, so here's the deal . . . .

If you've been married to someone for 10 years or more, then when you are social security eligible at age 62, as long as you've been divorced at least two years, if you're still working, and you haven't remarried, AND your ex reaches his full retirement age to qualify for social security, even if they are not actually taking it, you can start collecting your spousal benefit which is ½ of the benefit that your spouse would get if they took it at the same time.

Phew! That's a mouthful.

There are lots of caveats here to keep in mind. This won't work if you are remarried. If your own benefit would be more than your spousal benefit, then you would receive your own benefit. Bottom line there, if you work full time then your own benefit would be larger anyway so it doesn't matter.

In most cases, it usually makes the most sense to do nothing until you are FULL-retirement age. Congress passed legislation in October of 2015 that eliminated the file-and-suspend strategy so the spousal benefit is only going to be important to you if you haven't earned enough credits to get a larger payment on your own.

Now, keep in mind that whatever you decide to do has zero impact on your ex. He/she won't even be aware that you're taking anything.

Get this, let's say Bob marries wife 1 for 10 years and divorces. Bob does the same thing with wife 2, wife 3 and wife 4. Yep, he's a busy guy. Well guess what? ALL FOUR wives could collect a 50% spousal benefit based on Bob's earnings record. Is that the craziest thing you ever heard? No wonder the U.S. budget deficit is so high!

For good information on Social Security meet with a good CFP® or CDFA™ to make sure you understand your options and go to http://www.ssa.gov/planners/retire/divspo use.html

CHAPTER 10 – TAX ISSUES

Maintenance

Taxes just stink. But they stink really, really bad when you don't know they're coming! I hate it when a woman comes to me after having received alimony for about 11 months and didn't realize she was going to have to pay taxes on it come April 15th.

If you receive $60,000 in alimony, you will have a tax bill somewhere in the neighborhood of $10,000 – $15,000 depending on your situation. Ouch! So rule #1, if you receive alimony, know how much has to go into your tax savings account every month.

Filing Status

The IRS says that if you are legally divorced on Dec. 31 then you were single the whole year and you need to file taxes as single. If you are married on Dec. 31 then you either have to file married joint or married separate. If you can cooperate, it's almost always advantageous to file joint taxes but a good accountant will run it both ways for you and double check.

Let's talk about head of household. There is a huge tax advantage to being able to file using head of household as your status. You must meet all five of the criteria below to qualify:

- You did not file a joint tax return
- You paid more than half the cost of maintaining your home for the year
- Your spouse did not live in your home during the last six months of the year
- Your home was your child's main home for more than half of the year and your child qualifies as your dependent unless you gave up the exemption to your spouse
- You are a U.S. citizen or resident alien during the entire year

Now, if you have two or more children and you have substantially equal parenting time, you can BOTH claim head of household by alternating exemptions for the kids, meaning you each claim one child each year to meet the qualifications. This is always the way I suggest people set it up.

See the chapter on Alimony for more about the tax issues there.

Medical Expenses

Whoever pays the medical expenses for children or themselves gets to deduct the cost. Pretty simple.

Child Care Credit

Only one parent can take the child care credit. The IRS says it is the custodial parent.

Well, in Arizona, we no longer have a custodial parent in most cases. So then the IRS says it's whichever parent the child spent the most number of nights with and if that's equal, then it's the parent with the highest income.

Fair? Probably not. Regardless the person who claims the credit can only claim it for the dollars they actually paid.

Deductible Divorce Costs

Very few people realize you can actually deduct some of the costs of your divorce.

You can't deduct legal fees or court costs but you can deduct any fees, including legal, that were paid for tax advice related to the divorce or to get you spousal maintenance.

You should ask your attorney, mediator, and CDFA™ to break down their fees to show exactly what was billed related to tax advice or maintenance.

CHAPTER 11 – MANAGING YOUR FUTURE

Just when you think the worst is over and you've made it through the emotions, the fatigue, the fear, the anxiety, and you are finally on the other side, you realize that you now have to manage your finances on your own and they look VERY different than they did when you were married. Where do you even start to sort it all out? Can you afford to go to the movies this weekend? You're not even sure.

Unfortunately, the most common reaction to this situation is the old ostrich routine. "If I just pretend everything is ok, then it will be." Yeah . . . not so much.

So where do you start? Let me give you some tips to help you conquer the money demons and begin the next phase of your life with confidence and control.

1. **Start a Cash Flow Plan**
    That's my new term for budget. Don't get freaked out by the word "budget." I know that when you hear it you think "diet for my money" and that's not the case. A budget is the one and only way you can shift from unconscious spending to conscious choices that will lead to the outcomes you want.

    So instead of "diet" think "business plan." That's right; a budget is a "Business Plan for Money" that will guide you to financial success. There, now isn't that better?

    By the way, a budget is just a list of income and expenses and savings goals. There are TONS of budget tools online and a good financial advisor will be happy to help you get it set up. Even if you had a budget when you were married, toss it out. You need a new one reflective of your new reality.

2. Review Your Divorce Decree Thoroughly

One of the services I provide is post-divorce transition assistance and the first thing we do is go through the decree with a fine-tooth comb. (http://www.smarterdivorcesolutions.com/post-divorce-transition-assistance)

I have been STUNNED to discover that in about 75% of cases, there are assets that the client is entitled to that haven't been transferred and they didn't even realize they were supposed to get. Once your attorneys are done with your case and have the final judgment, they pretty much disappear leaving you to do all the tactical work of actually moving the assets around.

If you don't understand the legalese of your divorce decree, be sure you have an attorney or financial professional review it with you.

3. Create a Filing System

If you don't have one yet, now's the time to create a filing system next to the computer that you will use for your budgeting, online banking, etc. I'm a fan of old-fashion paper files so I still keep most of my stuff that way but I am starting to convert over to electronic.

My best advice for you is if you choose to go electronic, either a portable hard drive or cloud folder like Dropbox or Google Drive is essential. You don't want to wake up one day to a crashed computer and all your files are gone. People tell me that they worry about the security of these options. I choose not to dwell on it and just pay for an identity protection service. Life's too short to obsess over these things.

4. **Pay Yourself First**
   This is the most important step to securing your financial future. There is one simple thing that always separates the wealthy from the not so wealthy. ALL wealthy people live beneath their means – spend less than they make. It's a simple concept really but in the U.S. we are such a culture of instant gratification and

easy credit that we breed poor money habits like mosquitos in Mississippi.

It doesn't matter how much you make, the first 10% goes to pay yourself – period. If you just can't see how that could be possible, sit down with your financial advisor and discuss some choices. I promise you, it's possible.

5. **Hire an Advisor You Can Trust**
Even if you don't have a ton of assets, you need to hire an expert to help you with your planning and management. The money you spend will come back to you tenfold.

Even if you have financial experience and investing knowledge, if it's not your priority, you'll tend to ignore your investments when changes should be made and chances are you won't have a clear plan that you monitor annually either.

Trust me – find that partner you can trust. Interview them carefully and make sure you know EXACTLY how much you're paying in fees and what the industry averages are.

6. Remove Your Ex-Spouse's Name from Accounts

Go through your accounts and be sure to adjust the registrations. Pay special attention to any accounts that will be reporting to credit bureaus and any financial accounts. Retitle any vehicles in your name alone.

7. Establish Your Own Financial Identity

If you haven't already, get a credit card in your name as well as a checking and savings account. Start building your individual credit as soon as possible. Use the credit card but pay the full balance each month.

8. Notify All Insurance Policies

Be sure to review the beneficiaries on any policies and make sure that your ex-spouse's name is removed. Visit with your agent to be sure that you have all the coverage you need and that you understand all details of your policies.

If you're going to be using COBRA health coverage through your ex-spouse's employer, contact your insurer to find out how to set it up.

9. Write a New Will
Everything has changed. Be sure that your new wishes are clear so that there is no confusion.

10. Educate Yourself
You don't want to jump into major financial decisions before getting your bearings and making sure you fully understand the landscape. Many people find themselves in a situation where they are responsible for financial tasks that they never had to perform in their marriage. Take the time to educate yourself and understand your financial options. Seek out a financial expert who can help you grasp details of your money matters.

11. Notify Your Employer
Your employer may need to change company records, health or life insurance plans, and update accounts regarding 401K or retirement pro-

grams. You also need to fill out a new W-4 with your new tax filing status.

12. Revoke any Powers of Attorney

If you have given your former spouse a power of attorney you should ensure that it is revoked in writing. If the power of attorney was somehow recorded as part of a public record, a properly acknowledged revocation should be recorded as well.

13. Be Kind to Yourself

It will take at least a year to fully recover from your divorce. If you feel yourself struggling, don't hesitate to invest in a good therapist and be sure to put a strong support network in place.

Creating a New Relationship with Your Ex

At first, it's actually kind of exciting to think of a new and different friendship-based relationship with your ex. Then the emotions start and you'll undoubtedly find yourself on a roller coaster reminiscent of your adolescent puberty ride. Don't worry, you're not only normal, you're going through the process in a healthy way.

If you or your ex appear to be unaffected by the divorce, beware of emotional backlash down the road. The emotions of divorce can be resolved in one way and one way only: going THROUGH them. You can't stuff them down and hope they go away. They won't. So allow yourself to feel everything. Bless it and let it go.

If you have children together, just know and accept that you must have a relationship with your ex forever. I know, I know, you thought you were divorcing but if you have kids, you are connected for life. Your kids NEED you to be polite to each other and continue to co-parent.

My ex, unfortunately, has chosen not to do that and I've witnessed firsthand the negative impact on my children. It's not pretty and I'm sure they have years of therapy in their futures. I'm thinking of starting therapy funds for them instead of college funds. "Sorry honey, there's no money for college but I'd like you to meet with a friend of mine . . . . "(Sigh)

So ANYWAY – your ex. You decided that you found it impossible to live together; did you REALLY think that some magical thing would happen after divorce that would make it easier to communicate? Really? As Dr. Phil would say, "GET REAL!"

I promise you that if you had communication problems before, they will not only continue, they may get even worse. The key to communication with your ex is really quite simple, let go of expectations; ALL OF THEM. Do not need, want, demand, or expect ANYTHING from your ex. Trust me, you'll be much better off. Take the high road at every corner. Do and say what you KNOW is the right thing for your kids and let the rest go.

If you don't know the Serenity Prayer (http://www.cptryon.org/prayer/special/se renity.html) yet, now's the time to learn it. Repeat regularly and often. Treat your ex exactly the way you wish that they would treat you and you may discover the real miracle – they just might start doing it. But don't get your hopes up. Remember, no expectations. When you stop needing him/her to act in a certain way, you will truly find your personal freedom. And most importantly, your children will thrive.

My Final Wish for You

As our little tiptoe-through-the-tulips of divorce comes to an end, I want to leave you with a few words of encouragement.

Two years after my divorce, I did what every damaged, divorced woman over 40 does. I created a profile on Match.com of course. I was SO careful in writing my profile and even more careful in choosing who I would actually date. I went on dates with two men. Two years later I married one of them. (The other only lasted one date.)

Finding a mate in your 40's is VERY different than finding one in your 20's. This may not be true for everyone but I used the two years after my divorce to figure out who the hell I was. What did I want? What matters to me? What do I want the rest of my life to look like and who do I want to share it with? When I started to get clear on those things, I decided I was ready to date. And I attracted someone looking for exactly the same things.

Tom and I recently celebrated our fourth anniversary and I have to tell you, I never in my wildest dreams imagined that an intimate relationship could be completely effortless. He is my strongest supporter, my greatest fan, and everything I could ever have wanted. He makes me want to be a better woman so that I am deserving of what we share. There is life on the other side of divorce and it can be absolutely beautiful.

So I have a few new mottos in my life now that I share with those that are considering divorce:

If your marriage seems like really hard work, you are probably married to the wrong person.

You know you're with the right person when you become the best version of yourself.

When you're with the right person, you never feel belittled, misled, or ever have to censor what you say.

The right person appreciates your weaknesses as much as your strengths.

May you find the "right person" for you, if that's what you choose. In the meantime, explore your own space. Decide who you are, who you want to be, and who you want to share the journey with. Take your time. It's all we have anyway.

I wish you peace, healing, recovery, and abundance!

ABOUT THE AUTHOR

Nancy founded Smarter Divorce Solutions in 2011 after going through her own less-than-optimal divorce process. She has over 16 years of experience in both investment management and financial planning. In 2012 she joined Registered Investment Advisor firm Clarity Financial where she also provides full service financial planning and investment management.

She is a Master Analyst in Financial Forensics (MAFF™), a Certified Divorce Financial Analyst (CDFA™), an Accredited Wealth Management Advisor (AWMA), an

Accredited Asset Management Specialist (AAMS), a Chartered Mutual Fund Counselor (CMFC) and a trained mediator.

Nancy holds the Phoenix, 2015 Business Owner of the Year award from the National Association of Women Business Owners, was a 2014 Finalist in the BBB Business Ethics Awards, and is a frequent volunteer for the Fresh Start Foundation for Women.

For more information or to contact Nancy please visit her website at:

www.SmarterDivorceSolutions.com

APPENDIX A: BUDGET WORKSHEET

Note: If you would like copies of these worksheets to use, downloadable versions are available at my website:

www.SmarterDivorceSolutions.com/Divorceisnotfordummies

MONTHLY INCOME

Employment Income	$	2,500.00
Other Income	$	5,000.00
Other Income		

MONTHLY EXPENSES

Rent/mortgage	$	1,000.00
Electric	$	500.00
Gas		
Cell phone		
Internet/Cable		
Pool Service		
Yard Maintenance		
Student loans		
Credit cards	$	50.00
Water/Trash		
General Home Repairs		
House cleaning	$	2,000.00
Miscellaneous		
Other		

Food

Groceries	$	1,000.00
Dining Out		
Other		

Transportation

Car Payment	
Car Insurance	
Fuel	
Repair/Maintenance	
Other	

Clothing Expenses

Clothing	
Laundry/Dry Cleaning	

Medical

Insurance	
Prescriptions	
Holistice Healing	
Other	

Child Related Expenses

Education/Tuition	
Child Care	
Sports/Camps/Lessons	
Clothing	
Medical	
Dental/Orthodonics	
Optometry/Glasses/Contacts	
Prescriptions	
Allowances	
Miscellaneous	

Miscellaneous

Entertainment	
Hobbies	
Vacation/Travel	
Personal Care	
Toiletries	
Donations	
Pet Care	
Memberships/Clubs	
Child Support/Alimony	
Professional Fees	
Other	
Other	

Total Income	**$ 7,500.00**	
Total Expenses	**$ 4,550.00**	
Remaining Cash Available	**$ 2,950.00**	
Support Needed	**$**	**-**

APPENDIX B: ASSEMBLING THE FACTS

This document will help you assemble the list of all of the things that will be needed to complete your divorce process. For every item listed, if you and your spouse are mediating or doing your divorce yourself, you will need a copy of the most recent statement. If you are litigating or not cooperating well, you will need the last 3 months at a minimum and as much as 3 years of statements. For convenience, a cloud-sharing service like Dropbox or Google Drive is highly recommended for document storage. Assembling these documents now could save significant attorney fees later.

Assets

Bank Accounts				
Description	Value/ Date	Interest Rate	Checking/ Savings	Joint/or Individual

Investment Accounts NON-retirement				
Description	Value/ Date	Cost Basis	Type of Account	Joint/or Individual

Retirement Accounts				
Description	Value/ Date	Cost Basis	Type of Account**	Date Started if before marriage

**IRA, SEP IRA, Simple IRA, Roth IRA, 401(k), 403(b), Pension, Deferred compensation, etc.

Real Estate			
Basic Information	1st Property	2nd Property	3rd Property
Address:			
Current Value			
Original Cost			
Name(s) on Title			
1st Mortgage Balance:			
Interest Rate			
Monthly Payment (Principal and Interest Only)			
As of What Date			
What is the Plan?			
2nd Mortgage			
Balance:			
Interest Rate			
Monthly Payment (Principal and Interest Only)			
As of What Date			
What is the Plan?			

Life Insurance/Annuities

Description	Cash Value	Premium Paid by Party #1	Premium Paid by Party #2	Who's Insured?

Businesses

Description	Current Value	Original Cost	Annual Cash Flow	Legal Form (corp, sole prop, MLP)	How is it Titled?

Note: will need 3 years of Balance Sheets, Income Statements, Profit & Loss reports, and Tax Returns

Personal Items of Value

Vehicles						
Make/Model	Value	Loan Balance	Interest Rate	Monthly Payment	Current Mileage	Who's Keeping?

Family Heirlooms		
Description	Value	Who's Keeping?

Household Items		
Description	Value	Who's Keeping?

Liabilities (debts)

Description	Current Balance	Interest Rate	Monthly Payment

APPENDIX C: STATE BY STATE CHARTS

State Bar Associations

State	Bar Association Website
American Bar Association	www.abanet.org
Alabama	www.alabar.org
Alaska	www.alaskabar.org
Arizona	www.azbar.org
Arkansas	www.arkbar.com
California	www.calbar.org
Colorado	www.cobar.org
Connecticut	www.ctbar.org
Delaware	www.dsba.org
District of Columbia	www.badc.org, www.dcbar.org
Florida	www.flabar.org
Georgia	www.gabar.org
Hawaii	www.hsba.org
Idaho	www.isb.idaho.gov
Illinois	www.illinoisbar.org
Indiana	www.inbar.org

Iowa	www.iowabar.org
Kansas	www.ksbar.org
Kentucky	www.kybar.org
Louisiana	www.lsba.org
Maine	www.mainebar.org
Maryland	www.msba.org
Massachusetts	www.massbar.org
Michigan	www.michbar.org
Minnesota	www.mnbar.org
Mississippi	www.msbar.org
Missouri	www.mobar.org
Montana	www.montanabar.org
Nebraska	www.nebar.org
Nevada	www.nvbar.org
New Hampshire	www.nhbar.org
New Jersey	www.njsba.org
New Mexico	www.nmbar.org
New York	www.nysba.org
North Carolina	www.ncbar.org
North Dakota	www.sband.org
Ohio	www.ohiobar.org
Oklahoma	www.okbar.org
Oregon	www.osbar.org
Pennsylvania	www.pabar.org

Rhode Island	www.ribar.org
South Carolina	www.scbar.org
South Dakota	www.sdbar.org
Tennessee	www.tba.org
Texas	www.texasbar.org
Utah	www.utahbar.org
Vermont	www.vtbar.org
Virginia	www.vba.org
Washington	www.wsba.org
West Virginia	www.wvbar.org
Wisconsin	www.wisbar.org
Wyoming	www.wyomingbar.org

Grounds for Divorce

State	No Fault Only	No Fault and Fault Grounds	Residency Requirement
Alabama		Yes	6 months
Alaska		Yes	None
Arizona		Yes	90 days
Arkansas		Yes	60 days
California	Yes		6 months
Colorado	Yes		90 days
Connecticut		Yes	1 year
Delaware		Yes	6 months
District of Columbia	Yes		6 months
Florida	Yes		6 months
Georgia		Yes	6 months
Hawaii	Yes		6 months
Idaho		Yes	6 weeks
Illinois		Yes	90 days
Indiana		Yes	6 months
Iowa	Yes		None/1 year Petitioner
Kansas		Yes	60 days
Kentucky	Yes		180 days
Louisiana		Yes	6 months
Maine		Yes	6 months
Maryland		Yes	1 year
Massachusetts		Yes	1 year
Michigan	Yes		6 months
Minnesota	Yes		6 months
Mississippi		Yes	6 months
Missouri		Yes	90 days
Montana	Yes		90 days
Nebraska	Yes		1 year
Nevada		Yes	6 weeks
New		Yes	1Year

Hampshire			
New Jersey		Yes	1 year
New Mexico		Yes	6 months
New York		Yes	1 year
North Carolina		Yes	6 months
North Dakota		Yes	6 months
Ohio		Yes	6 months
Oklahoma		Yes	6 months
Oregon	Yes		6 months
Pennsylvania		Yes	6 months
Rhode Island		Yes	1 year
South Carolina		Yes	1 year/3 months if both
South Dakota		Yes	None
Tennessee		Yes	6 months
Texas		Yes	6 months
Utah		Yes	3 months
Vermont		Yes	6 months
Virginia		Yes	6 months
Washington	Yes		None
West Virginia		Yes	1 year
Wisconsin	Yes		6 months
Wyoming		Yes	60 days

Property Division

State	Property Distribution	Property Model	Increase in Value of Separate Property
Alabama	Equitable	None	Separate
Alaska	Equitable	All Property	Marital
Arizona	Community Property	Dual Property	Separate
Arkansas	Equitable	Dual Property	Separate
California	Community Property	Dual Property	Separate
Colorado	Equitable	Dual Property	Marital
Connecticut	Equitable	All Property	Marital
Delaware	Equitable	Dual Property	Separate
District of Columbia	Equitable	Dual Property	Separate
Florida	Equitable	Dual Property	Separate
Georgia	Equitable	Dual Property	Separate
Hawaii	Equitable	All Property	Marital
Idaho	Community Property	Dual Property	Separate
Illinois	Equitable	Dual Property	Separate
Indiana	Equitable	All Property	Marital
Iowa	Equitable	All Property	Marital
Kansas	Equitable	All Property	Marital

Kentucky	Equitable	Dual Property	Separate
Louisiana	Community Property	Dual Property	Separate
Maine	Equitable	Dual Property	Separate
Maryland	Equitable	Dual Property	Separate
Massachusetts	Equitable	All Property	Marital
Michigan	Equitable	All Property	Marital
Minnesota	Equitable	Dual Property	Separate
Mississippi	Equitable	Dual Property	Separate
Missouri	Equitable	Dual Property	Separate
Montana	Equitable	All Property	Marital
Nebraska	Equitable	Dual Property	Separate
Nevada	Community Property	Dual Property	Marital
New Hampshire	Equitable	All Property	Marital
New Jersey	Equitable	Dual Property	Separate
New Mexico	Community Property	Dual Property	Marital
New York	Equitable	Dual Property	Separate
North Carolina	Equitable	Dual Property	Separate
North Dakota	Equitable	All Property	Marital
Ohio	Equitable	Dual Property	Separate
Oklahoma	Equitable	Dual Property	Separate

Oregon	Equitable	All Property	Marital
Pennsylvania	Equitable	Dual Property	Marital
Rhode Island	Equitable	Dual Property	Separate
South Carolina	Equitable	Dual Property	Separate
South Dakota	Equitable	All Property	Marital
Tennessee	Equitable	Dual Property	Separate
Texas	Community Property	Dual Property	Separate
Utah	Equitable	All Property	Marital
Vermont	Equitable	All Property	Marital
Virginia	Equitable	Dual Property	Separate
Washington	Community Property	Dual Property	Separate
West Virginia	Equitable	Dual Property	Separate
Wisconsin	Community Property	Dual Property	Separate
Wyoming	Equitable	All Property	Marital